Before They Were Famous

Dolly Parton

Written by Stephen Krensky
Illustrated by Bobbie Houser

A Crabtree Crown Book

Crabtree Publishing
crabtreebooks.com

School-to-Home Support for Caregivers and Teachers

This book is designed to teach and appeal to a student on core subject areas. The student will build upon what they already know about the subject and engage in topics that they do not know but want to learn more about. Here are a few guiding questions to help the reader on his or her comprehension skills. Possible answers appear here in red.

Before Reading:

What do I know about this topic?

- *I know that Dolly Parton is a famous country music performer and songwriter.*
- *I know that Dolly Parton built Dollywood so that the people who lived in the area would have good paying jobs working there.*

What do I want to learn about this topic?

- *I want to learn more about the years Dolly spent singing at the Grand Ole Opry.*
- *I want to learn more about the songs Dolly wrote before she moved to Nashville.*

During Reading:

I'm curious to know...

- *I'm curious to know how old Dolly was when she started to sing in public at her grandfather's church.*
- *I'm curious to know how Dolly comes up with ideas for her songs.*

How is this like something I already know?

- *I know that other singers got their start in the music business by singing in churches.*
- *I know that a lot of famous country singers got their start by appearing at the Grand Ole Opry.*

After Reading:

What was the author trying to teach me?

- *I think the author was trying to teach me that you must have perseverance and never quit when you have a dream for yourself to achieve great things.*
- *I think the author was trying to teach me that although you may come from a poor family you can achieve great things in life.*

How did the photographs and captions help me understand more?

- *I didn't know that at age seven Dolly Parton made her first guitar from an old mandolin and two guitar strings.*
- *I didn't know that Dolly first heard recorded music while sitting around the radio listening with her family.*

Table of Contents

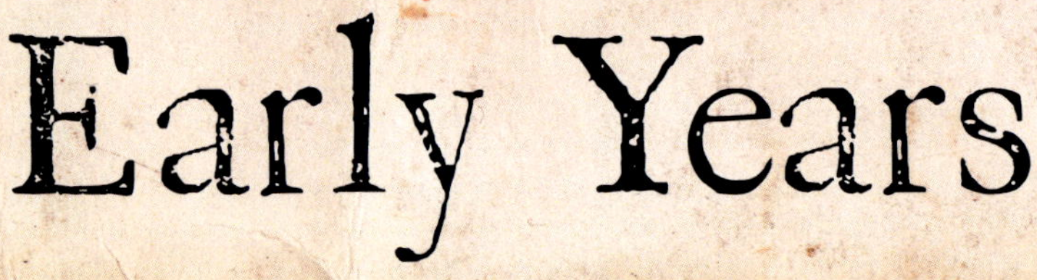

Early Years

The country church looked like a very big place. And all the people filling it up made it look even bigger.

The little girl standing at the front didn't mind that. Her grandfather was the **preacher** in that church. And soon he would be speaking again to the congregation. But for now, everyone was looking at the little girl with blond curls and green eyes. And that suited her just fine.

Six-year-old Dolly Parton was about to sing.

Dolly Parton

Fun Facts

In addition to his preaching, Dolly's grandfather, Jake Robert Owens, also wrote and performed music.

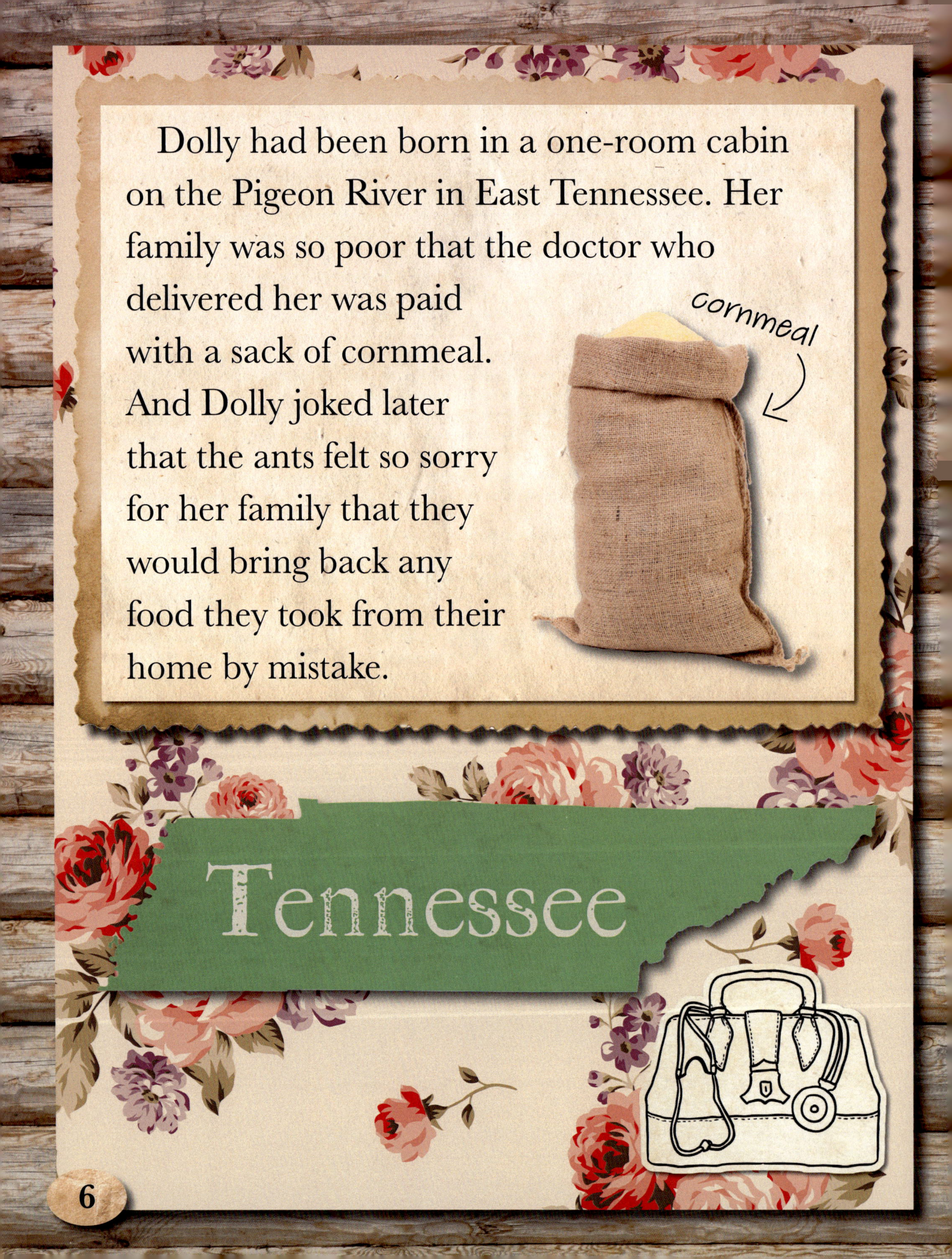

Dolly had been born in a one-room cabin on the Pigeon River in East Tennessee. Her family was so poor that the doctor who delivered her was paid with a sack of cornmeal. And Dolly joked later that the ants felt so sorry for her family that they would bring back any food they took from their home by mistake.

replica of Dolly Parton's childhood Smoky Mountain home

Fun Facts

Dolly's first home didn't have electricity, running water, or an indoor bathroom.

Making Music

Dolly was the fourth of twelve children, six boys and six girls. Her father Lee was a **sharecropper**, farming someone else's land in return for a share of the crops. But not a very large share.

Dolly

Her mother Avie Lee came from a musical family. She often sang old folk songs as she went about her household chores. And with twelve children to care for, she never ran out of reasons to sing.

Fun Facts

Dolly loved to read so much that she would read anything and everything she could find, from the Bible to old newspaper pages that were stuffed into the house walls for insulation.

Music was one of the best things about Dolly's life.

"Ever since I was a small child," she wrote later, "I've always had the gift to rhyme. So, I was making up songs before I could even write. I would rhyme everything, whether it was whatever was on the table, what was on the floor, what the kids were doing."

Fun Facts

Dolly and her family once survived a tornado that wiped out the land and most of the animals nearby, but left her family safe inside their cabin.

Dolly put music and words together for the first time when she was about six. It was a song in honor of her **corncob** doll named Tasseltop.

"Little Tiny Tasseltop," it began, "I love you an awful lot."

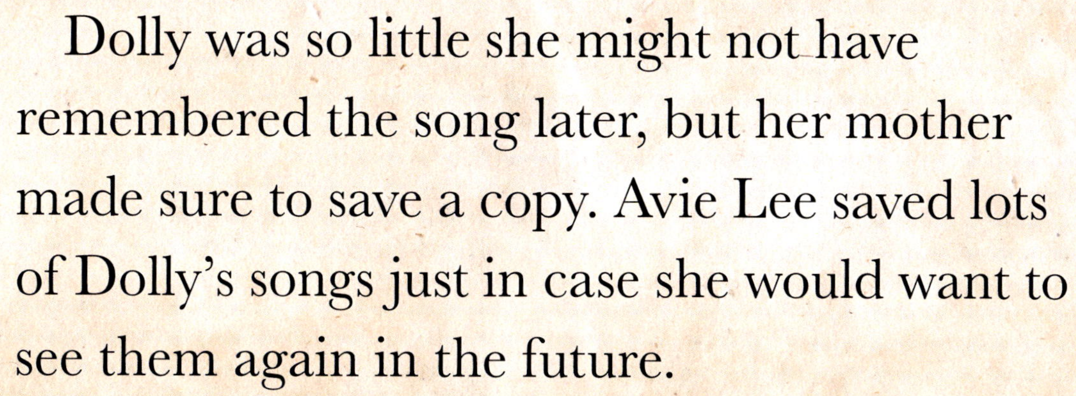

Dolly was so little she might not have remembered the song later, but her mother made sure to save a copy. Avie Lee saved lots of Dolly's songs just in case she would want to see them again in the future.

Fun Facts

Dolly's mother made Dolly a coat from different scraps of cloth. The kids at school made fun of it, but the coat inspired Dolly later to write the song "Coat of Many Colors" almost twenty years later.

As much as Dolly liked to sing, she wanted to play instruments, too. At seven she made herself a guitar from an old **mandolin** and two leftover guitar strings.

The next year, her Uncle Lewis, seeing how serious she was about music, gave her his own Martin guitar.

"It was my treasure," Dolly remembered later.

Fun Facts

Dolly's favorite guitars became the Taylor GS Mini and the Martin 5-18. She can actually play around twenty instruments.

On Saturday nights, Dolly and her family sat around and listened to songs on their battery-powered radio. They joined millions of people who were enjoying recorded music they would never have been able to hear otherwise.

Country music stars like Hank Williams, Kitty Wells, and Bill Munroe reached a national audience of millions that earlier performers could only dream about.

Fun Facts

WSM Radio, home of the Grand Ole Opry, first went on the air in 1925. By the 1940s the radio station could be heard in most of the eastern and central United States.

Stepping Up

Dolly herself was soon performing on the radio, too. At ten, another uncle, Bill, encouraged her to appear on the *Cas Walker Show*. This was a **variety** program that helped promote a chain of grocery stores. The show wasn't fancy or **glamorous**, but it was a big change from just singing at home with her brothers and sisters.

Dolly Parton

Dolly dedicated herself to appearing with Cas Walker as often as possible — afternoons after school, during the summer, and on holidays.

Fun Facts

Dolly was a big hit with the crowd in her first *Cas Walker* appearance. She ended up singing the same song several times to make them happy.

At thirteen, Dolly recorded a single called "Puppy Love" for a small recording **label** in Louisiana. "That record didn't do anything," she recalled later, "because it wasn't good at all! But it was a start, and I had big dreams."

Fun Facts

Dolly wrote “Puppy Love” when she was eleven. It took her thirty hours on a bus to get to the recording studio in Lake Charles, Louisiana.

A Bigger Stage

The biggest dream a country singer could have was the chance to appear at the Grand Ole Opry. Founded in 1925, the Opry featured weekly concerts from its home in Nashville, Tennessee. These concerts were broadcast on the radio, and **aspiring** country singers waited, sometimes for years, for a chance to perform.

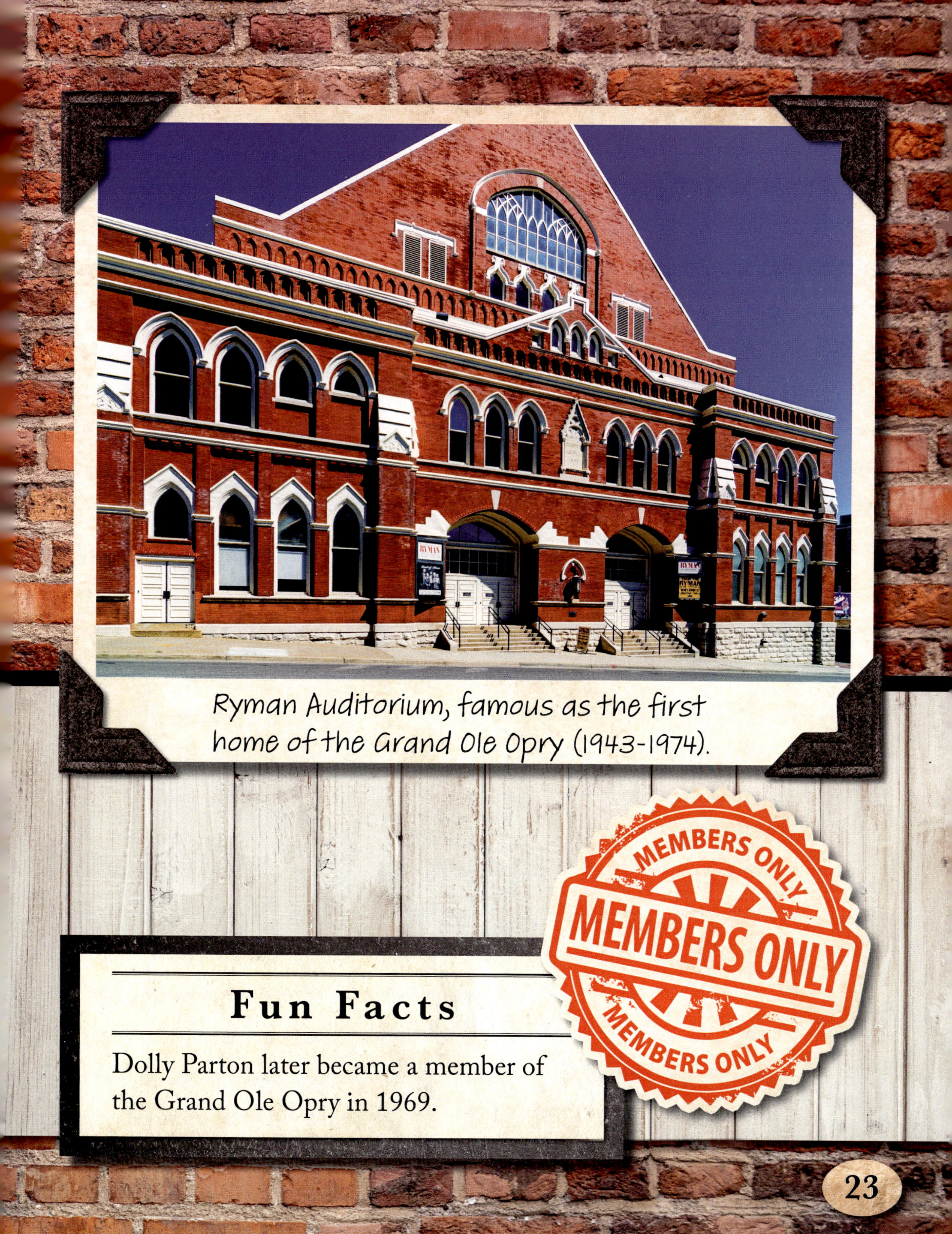

Ryman Auditorium, famous as the first home of the Grand Ole Opry (1943-1974).

Fun Facts

Dolly Parton later became a member of the Grand Ole Opry in 1969.

Dolly Parton made her first appearance at the Grand Ole Opry in 1959 when she was thirteen. Country music star Johnny Cash introduced her, saying, "We've got a little girl here from up in East Tennessee. Her daddy's listening to the radio at home, and she's gonna be in real trouble if she doesn't sing tonight, so let's bring her out here."

Johnny Cash

Fun Facts

"You Gotta Be My Baby" was written by country singer George Jones. He recorded and released the song in 1956.

Dolly with her uncle, Bill Owens.

Dolly stood alongside her uncle, Bill Owens, and sang a song called, "You Gotta Be My Baby." The audience was so taken with her that she sang three **encores** before finally leaving the stage.

On the Move

In high school Dolly joined the band and played the drums. But she still spent most of her free time sitting at a piano and writing songs.

And as soon as she graduated in 1964, Dolly moved to Nashville, promoting herself first as a songwriter rather than as a singer.

Fun Facts

On Dolly's first day in Nashville, she met her future husband, Carl Dean. They have been married for over fifty years.

But Dolly's good looks, angelic voice, and heartfelt songs would not keep her in the background for long. In 1967, country music superstar Porter Wagoner made her a regular on his television show.

There was no stopping her after that. As Dolly herself said later, "You'll never do a whole lot unless you're brave enough to try."

Porter Wagoner Dolly

Fun Facts

Dolly Parton wrote the song "I Will Always Love You," in honor of Porter Wagoner. It became her biggest hit when performed by Whitney Houston in 1992.

Dolly Parton was born in the Great Smoky Mountains of East Tennessee on January 16, 1946. Her first home was a one-room cabin with no electricity or running water. Her musical career grew rapidly after high school, leading to three #1 hits in the early 1970s. She then expanded her entertainment ventures into acting and producing.

Besides her many musical achievements, Dolly opened Dollywood, an entertainment-based theme park in 1986. Her plan was both to honor the heritage of the Great Smoky Mountains and to create a new source of lasting jobs for the people who lived there. She has also supported many charitable efforts, especially Dolly Parton's Imagination Library, which distributes a free book every month to young children around the world.

In addition to her many talents, Dolly has always brought to her life an ongoing sense of focus and confidence. "Find out who you are," Dolly has said proudly, "and do it on purpose."

GLOSSARY

aspiring
Having ambition to achieve a specific goal

corncob
The central part of an ear of corn without the kernels

encores
Additional performances made in response to applause

glamorous
Beautiful in a dressed-up way

label
A company that produces records

mandolin
A stringed instrument with a pear-shaped body and a long neck

preacher
A minister of a Christian religion

sharecropper
A farmer who rents land for farming and pays the rent with some of the crops raised

variety
A collection of different things from a larger common group

INDEX

COMPREHENSION QUESTIONS

What was the name of Dolly's corncob doll?

Who introduced Dolly for her first appearance at the Grand Ole Opry?

What instrument did Dolly play in her high school band?

ABOUT THE AUTHOR

Stephen Krensky is the award-winning author of more than 150 fiction and nonfiction books for children. He and his wife Joan live in Lexington, Massachusetts, and he happily spends as much time as possible with his grown children and not-so-grown grandchildren.

Written by: Stephen Krensky

Illustrations by: Bobbie Houser

Designed by: Bobbie Houser

Series Development: James Earley

Proofreader: Kathy Middleton

Educational Consultant: Marie Lemke M.Ed.

Production manager: Candice Campbell

Photographs:

t = Top, c = Center, b = Bottom, l = Left, r = Right

Alamy: Pictorial Press: cover bl, p. 24; Media Punch: p. 5 t, 8 r, 18; Stephen Saks Photography: p. 7 c; Pictorial Press Ltd: p. 15 bl; Historic Collection: p. 17 cr; Cindy Miller Hopkins/ DanitaDelimont.com: p. 22; Danny Hooks: p. 23 t; Archive PL: p. 28; dollyparton.com: p. 25 t; p. 27 cr; Shutterstock: Olha Turchenko: cover tl; AlexMaster: cover br, p. 5 b; BCFC: p. 4 c; AVA Bitter: p. 4 r, 13 bl; indigolotos: p. 6 t; imagestockdesign: p. 6 c; Line and Circle: p. 6 br; Callahan: p. 7 tr; Amanda. Reynolds: p. 7 bl; Canicula: p. 8 bl; Black Creator 24: p. 9 r; magicoven: p. 9 l; chrisdorney: p. 11 tl; Minerva Studio: p. 11 c; patrimonio designs ltd: p. 11 bl; Sarycheva Olesia: p. 12 bl; JosepPerianes: p. 13 tr; dean bertoncelj: p. 15 tr, 27 cl; ArtMari: p. 15 cl; Dalibor Sevaljevic: p. 16 tr; Maxx-Studio: p. 17 tr; dobrograph: p. 17 bl; Oxlock: p. 19 tr; Photology1971: p. 20 tr, 26 b; TeddyandMia: p. 21 tl; blinkblink: p. 21 c; RetroClipArt: p. 21 br; astudio: p. 23 br, 27 tl; Rita Owl: p. 25 cr; Nosyrevy: p. 25 b; alya_haciyeva: p. 27 tc; Macrovector: p. 27 b; mhatzapa: p. 29 t; Tinseltown: p. 29 br

Crabtree Publishing

crabtreebooks.com 800-387-7650

Printed in the U.S.A./CP072026

Published in Canada Crabtree Publishing
616 Welland Ave.
St. Catharines, Ontario
L2M 5V6

Published in the United States Crabtree Publishing
347 Fifth Ave
Suite 1402-145
New York, NY 10016

Library and Archives Canada Cataloguing in Publication
Available at Library and Archives Canada

Library of Congress Cataloging-in-Publication Data
Available at the Library of Congress

Hardcover: 978-1-0398-3891-8
Paperback: 978-1-0398-3976-2
Ebook (pdf): 978-1-0398-4051-5
Epub: 978-1-0398-4123-9